Inner and Outer Space: Paintings and Poetry

TINA KARAGULIAN

Black Rose Arts & Press

San Antonio

Black Rose Arts & Press
San Antonio, Texas
www.tinakaragulian.com

Cover art is a photograph of an acrylic painting entitled *Rolling Silhouette* by Tina Karagulian.
Calibri is the selected font for this book.
Photograph of *Luminous* by Ron Johanningsmeier, reprinted with permission.
Photograph of author by Marcy Maloy, reprinted with permission. www.marcymaloy.com.
Layout, logo, and book design by Tina Karagulian.

Karagulian, Tina, 1965–

Inner and Outer Space *: Paintings and Poetry* / Art / Poetry/
Tina Karagulian

1. Art 2. Poetry 3. Spirituality

Printed in the United States of America on recycled paper.

ISBN:

978-0983804215

"As a young girl, I envisioned being the first girl on the moon. Within nature and within the far-reaches of space, I wanted to experience every reality firsthand. I learned that art and life invite us to make space for our inner creativity while honoring the creative lives of others. Over time, that dance of space challenged me to refashion acquired roles and identities, expanding to become more and more present to the threads of love and compassion within myself and within my world. This series of paintings and poetry invites exploration of the space we give to our inner and outer journeys."

Tina Karagulian

CONTENTS

ACKNOWLEDGMENTS

The majority of the paintings and poetry from this book come from an art exhibition at Intermezzo Gallery in Boerne, Texas from March through April of 2015. I am grateful for Kathy Cody Gallaway and Tom Gallaway for their invitation to showcase my artistry. I would also like to thank Ron Johanningsmeier for his photograph of my painting Luminous. And always, I thank Paschal Booker and Walden Sevart Booker for their unending support and inspiration.

Tina Karagulian

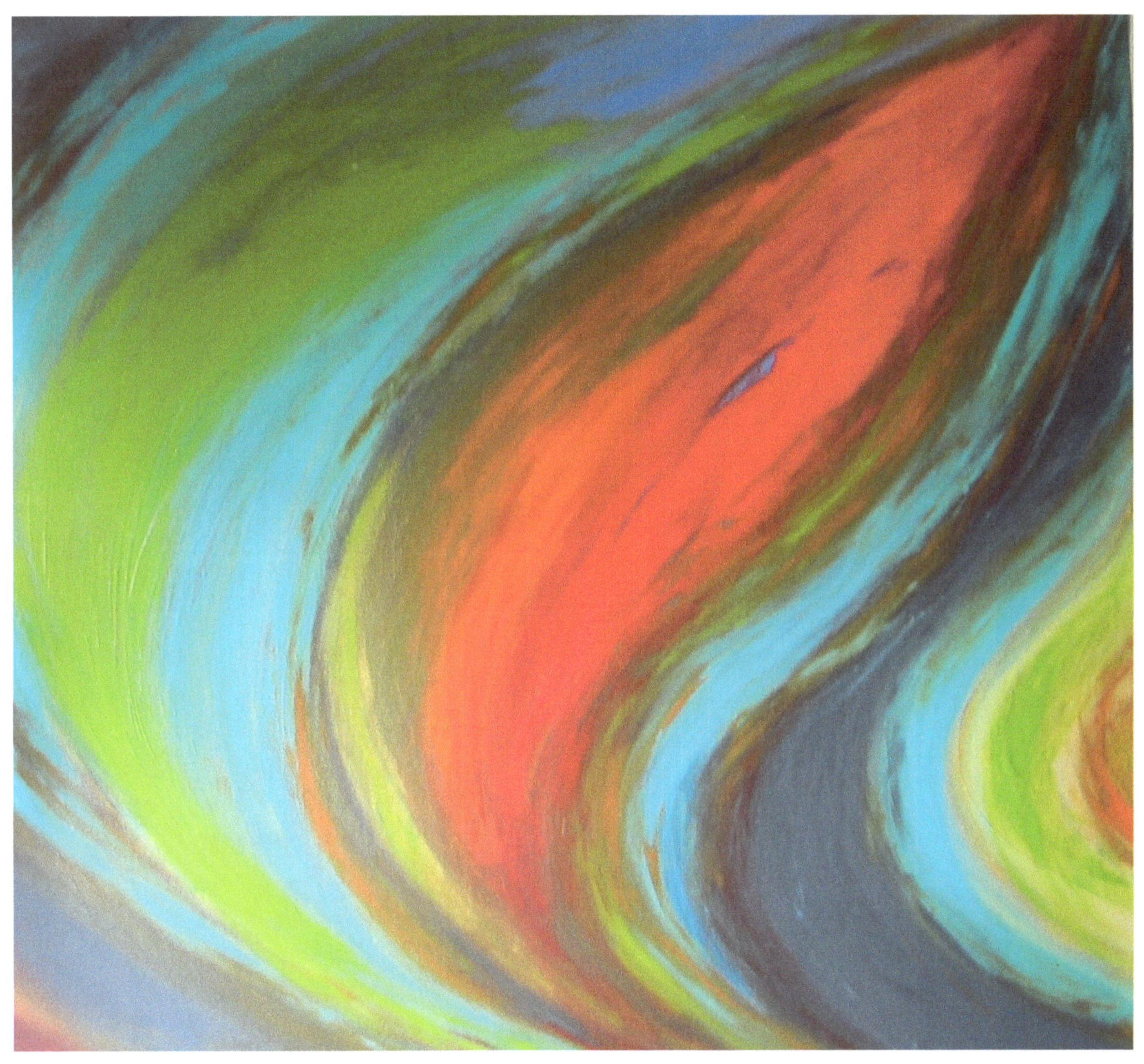

Celestial, acrylic on canvas, 36 x 36 inches

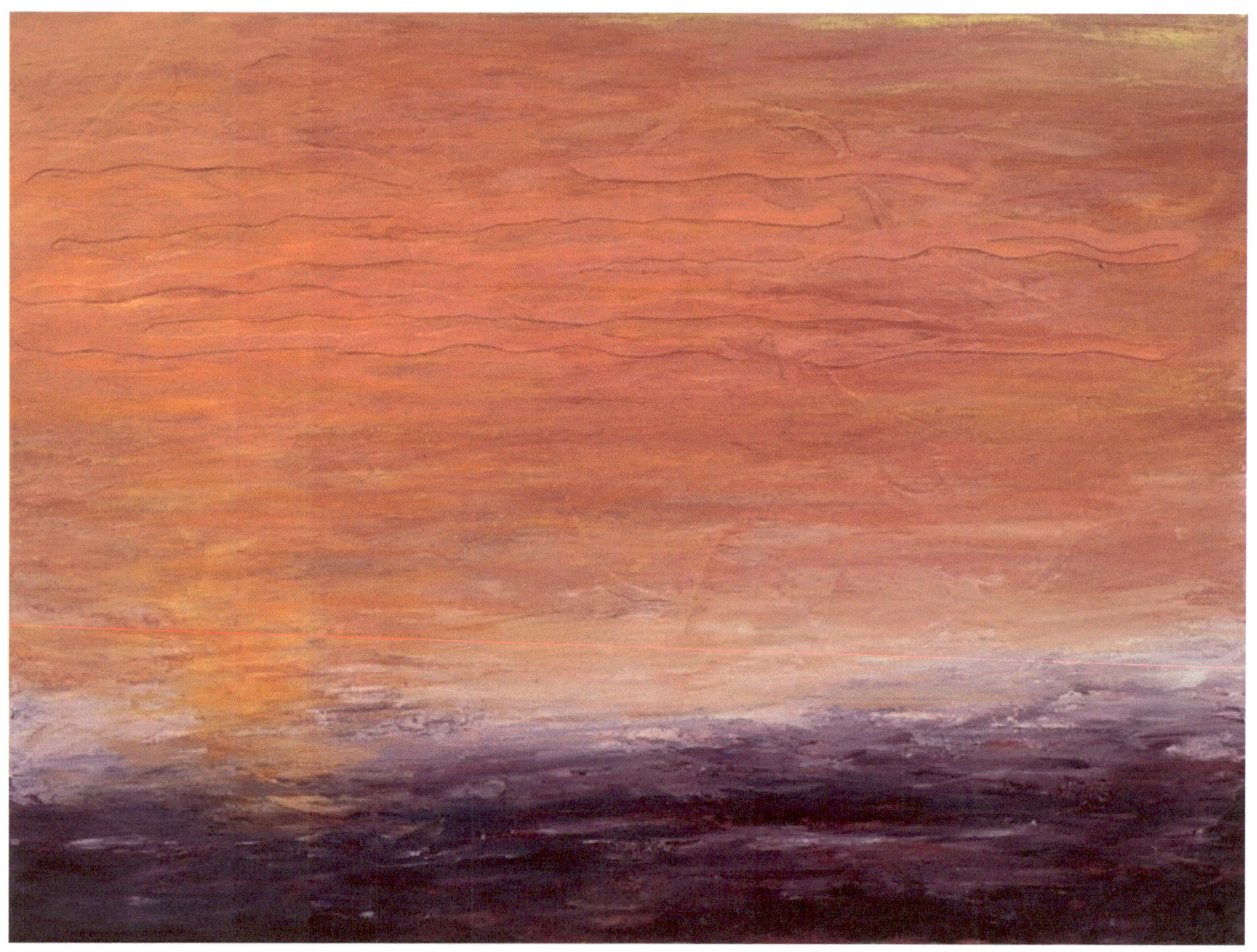

au coucher du soleil, acrylic on canvas, 30 x 40 inches

au coucher du soleil
(bedtime of the sun)

Trace the sun's descent,
dripping with colors
of the day's radiant glow,
the touch of water's kiss,
and the first, cool breath
of night's embrace.
Linger here,
melted sky into lapping wave,
buoyed by suns
that daily cast nets
of frolic and wisdom
upon unsuspecting hearts,
to savor the moment
and every waking tomorrow.

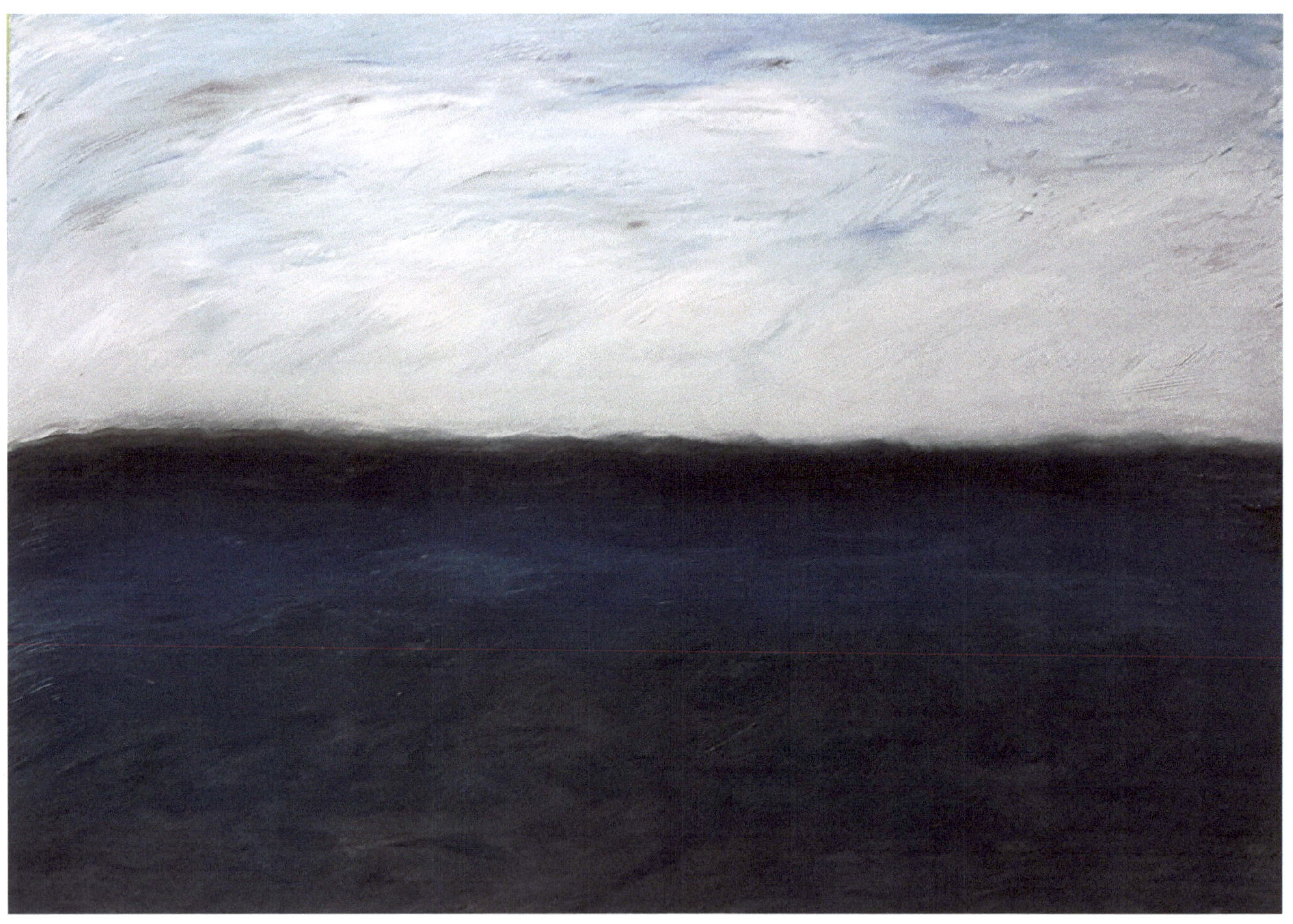

Cloudy Day, acrylic on canvas, 36 x 48 inches

Tina Karagulian

Clouds

Clouds move in unison,
like starlings in flight,
considering each turn
then changing direction,
led by inner pulse,
unseen by naked eye.

I watch the clouds of my life—
wisps of lightness
and dark brooding curves
that synchronize
into a steady unfolding,
a summon into rhythms
that know no outcome,
yet gather in surprise
of moment's gaze.

I learn to lean
into each forward movement,
gliding upon air currents
that uplift and embrace.

I become the cloud,

fingering the sky's canvas,
tasting the rain upon my lips,
as it showers down
for all who thirst.
I no longer ask
what moves mountains,
forms clouds,
or paints the sky.

Clouds never ask why.

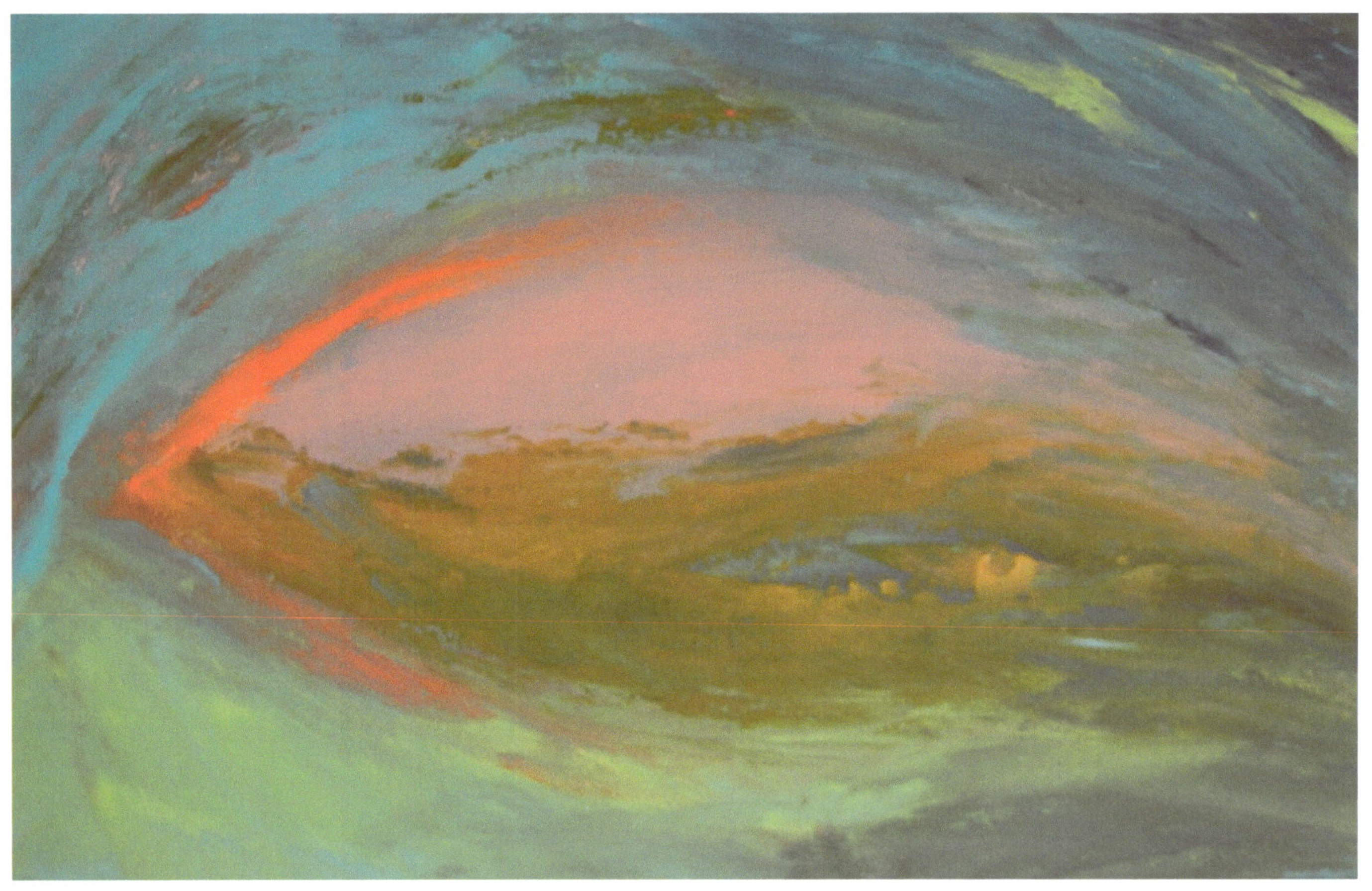

Resonance, acrylic on canvas, 12 x 24 inches

Clouds on the Bay

Notice the clouds
on the bay.
They fly above and
allow the sea
room to be,
each in its own world.
The sharing of water
is their bridge,
drops that feed the clouds,
which then rain into sea.
I wonder what they whisper
to one another
within each drop
of water passed
between them.
Their love affair
bends and moves
in a language all their own.
If we trust our own rhythms,
like they trust theirs,
we will understand
how love endures.

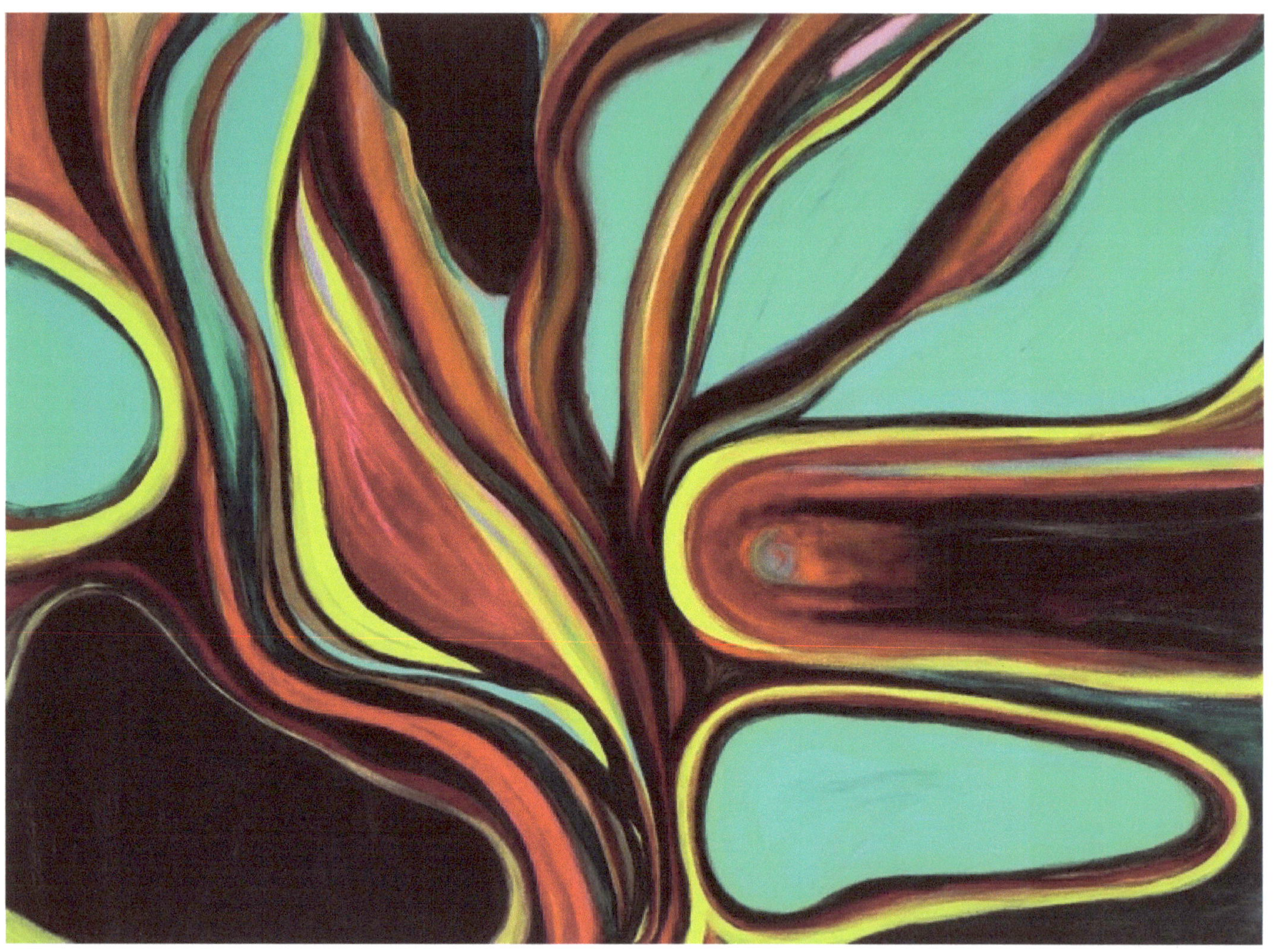

Coral Flight, acrylic on canvas, 30 x 40 inches

Coral Flight

This salsa,
Rumba,
waltz,
or cha cha,
whatever you name
this dance,
this life,
make the most
of every staccato,
sharp and flat,
loom in the crescendos
of every coral dream,
and before taking full flight,
become the intermezzo,
become the grace
in every note,
until you savor
all of life.

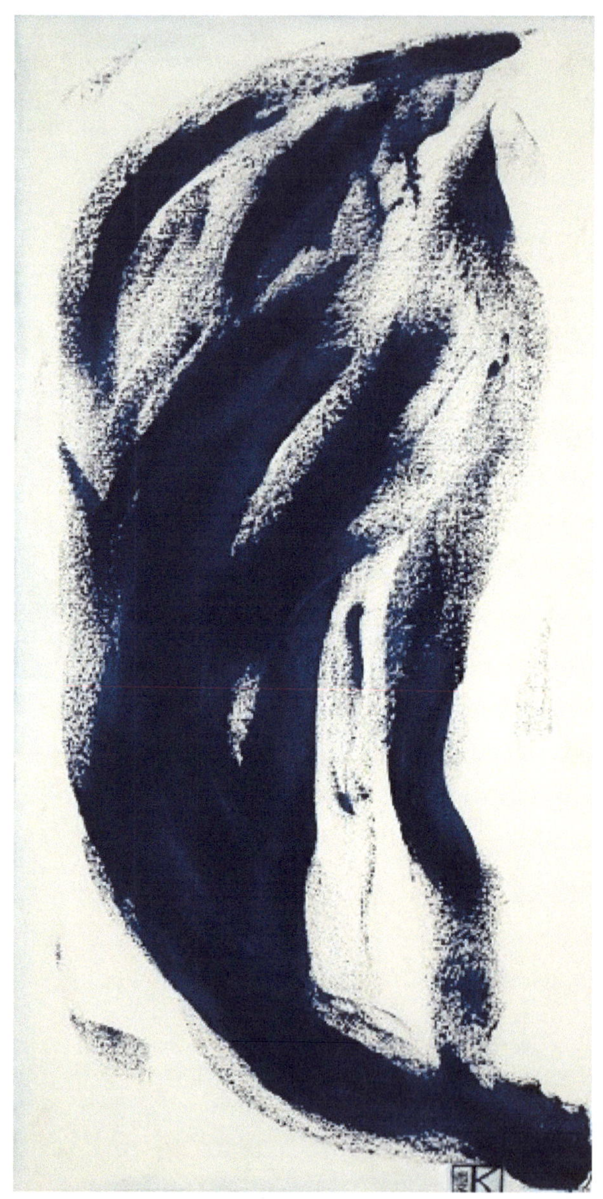

Abstract Blue, oil on canvas, 29.5 x 14.5 inches

Flow

The inner flow
and rhythm of you
invites toe, foot, then
leaps into winged flight,
glides upon silent air,
smiles through turbulent waters,
and lands softly upon fresh soil.
This beacon of light
carries our weary bodies
into the eye of storms
until our strong-held beliefs
crumble under raging waters
and become like passing mist.
The embers of life
are blown by inner blaze,
filling space
of hearts and worlds,
so that
all that moves,
all that we now see,
is the beauty
in each soul's yearning
to fully awaken and follow
a sacred rhythm,
where unworn paths bow down
to the ever-present mystery
flowing from our One, true heart.

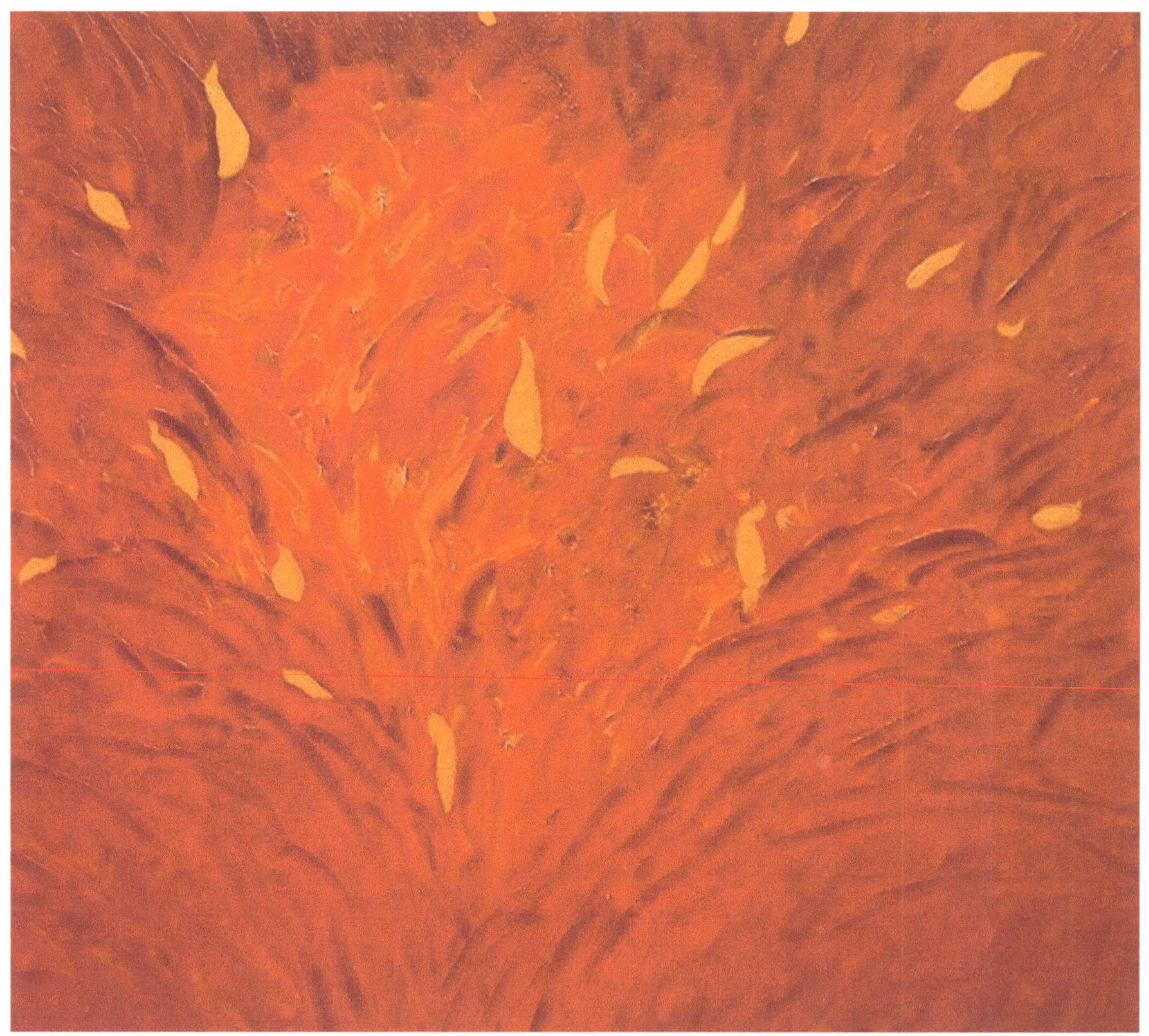

Opening, acrylic on canvas, 18 x 18 inches

Verdant Heart

Sweet is the haze
that falls gently upon day,
a reminder to tarry,
to drink the ease
of possibility,
warming the gold
of your verdant heart,
alive in whispers
that engage and bend
the creative yearning
of your crimson sun.
Reach into twilight,
along the ripple
that follows
in bird and boat's wake.
There,
and in still waters,
I wait.

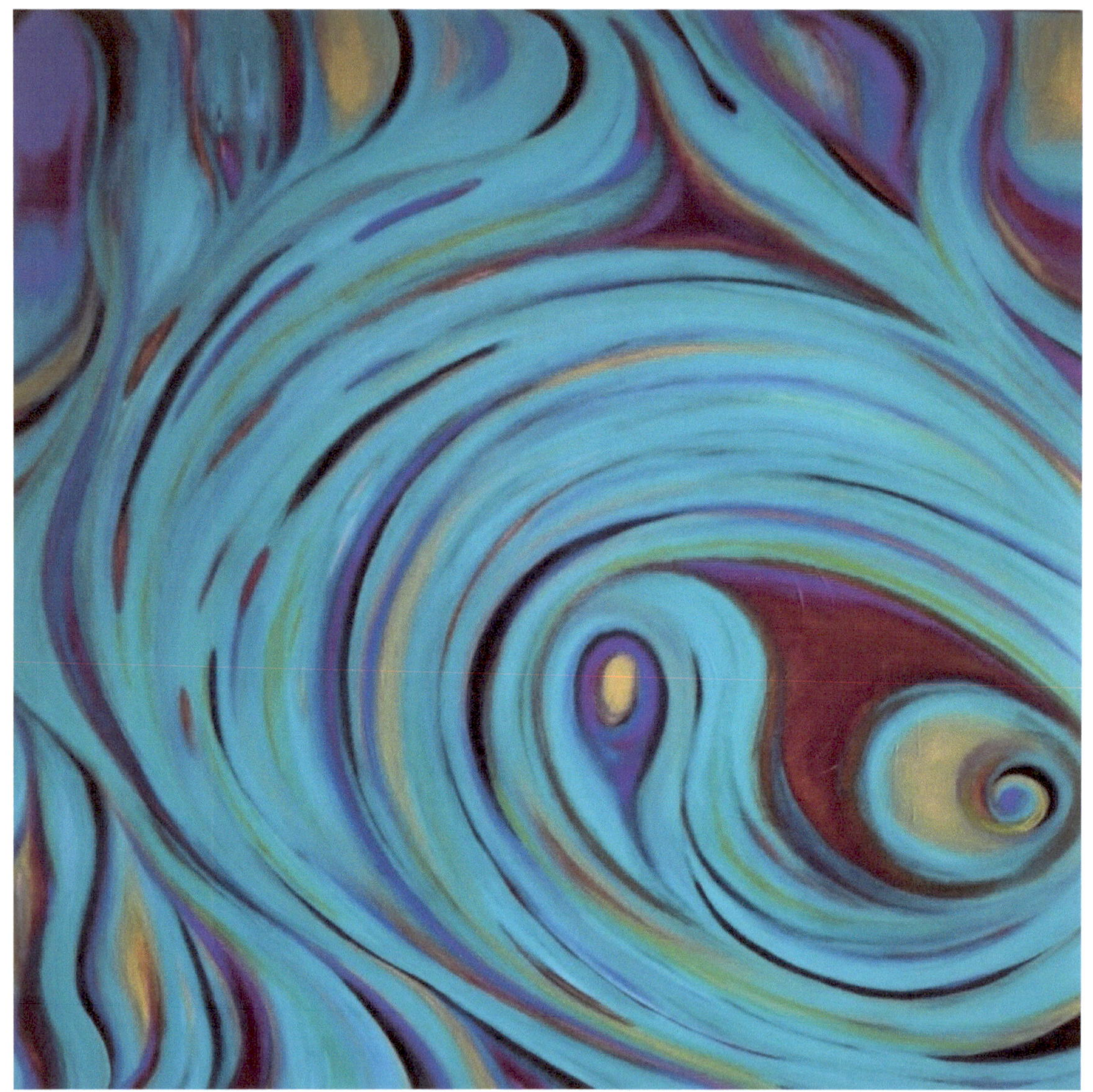

Luminous, acrylic on canvas, 48 x 48 inches

Luna Azul

Blue moon
whispers
as she curtsies,
leaving behind
her silvery veils,
to awaken
tonight's muse.

Luna Azul,*
walk with me,
infuse me with
the knowing
of many crones
that have danced
across the sky.

Gabooyd Lucine,**
ancestral moon,
soothe the silent lines
that bend upon the wave,
cup your hands
about my face,
spilling
incandescent
dreams
over
every
open
heart.

**Spanish* for Blue Moon
***Armenian* for Blue Moon

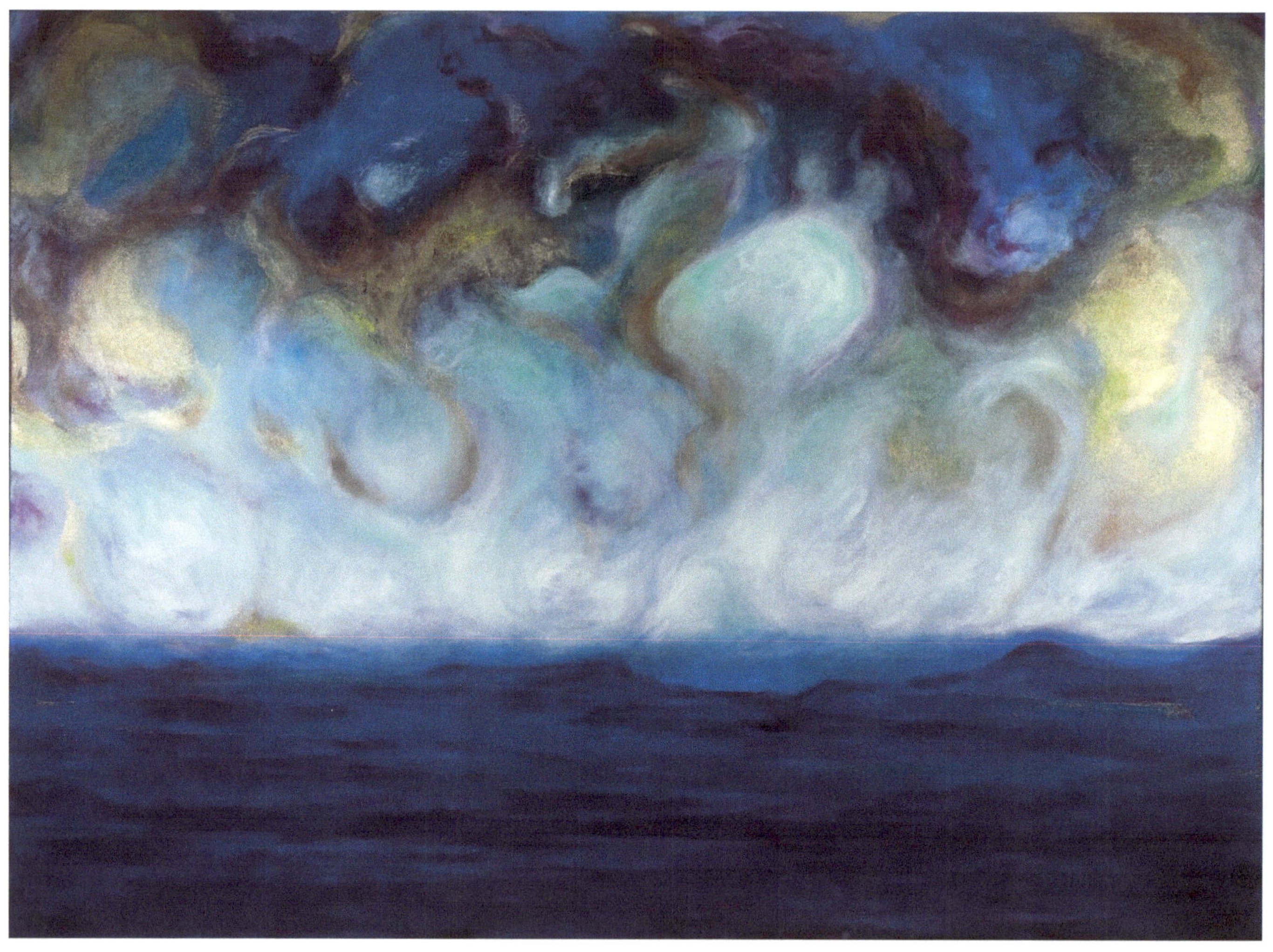

Ocean Nebula, acrylic on canvas, 30 x 40 inches

Ocean Nebula

Rising up,
bouncing lightly off waves,
I become mist,
watching shadows,
golden-violet blues
that meet in greening dawn.
I caress the sun,
become lover with sky, bird,
and curve of heaven,
then gently,
gently,
cascade down
as ocean rain.

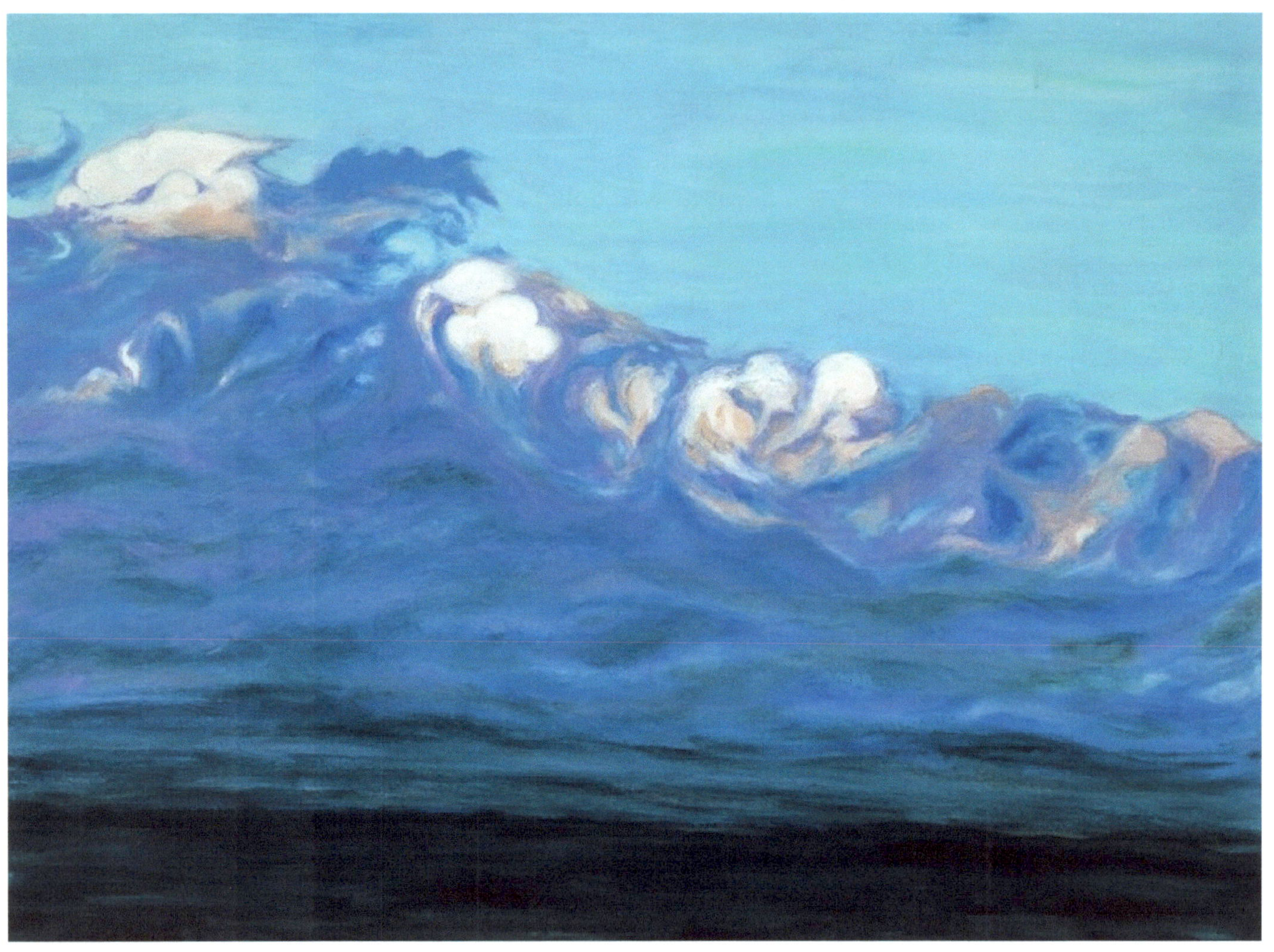

Rolling Silhouette, acrylic on canvas, 30 x 40 inches

Rolling Silhouette

I want to roll with the clouds,
tumble around the neighborhood,
amid sounds and colors of sky.

Those who fly,
whether wisp of cloud
or bird of wing,
know how to be,
how to become
light as a feather,
and laugh
until contentment
breathes a grateful sigh.
I want to glide
on currents of air,
bask in the moon's loving stare,
and reflect the dreams
that stars ignite.

Wanna roll with the clouds?
Let's rumble tonight!

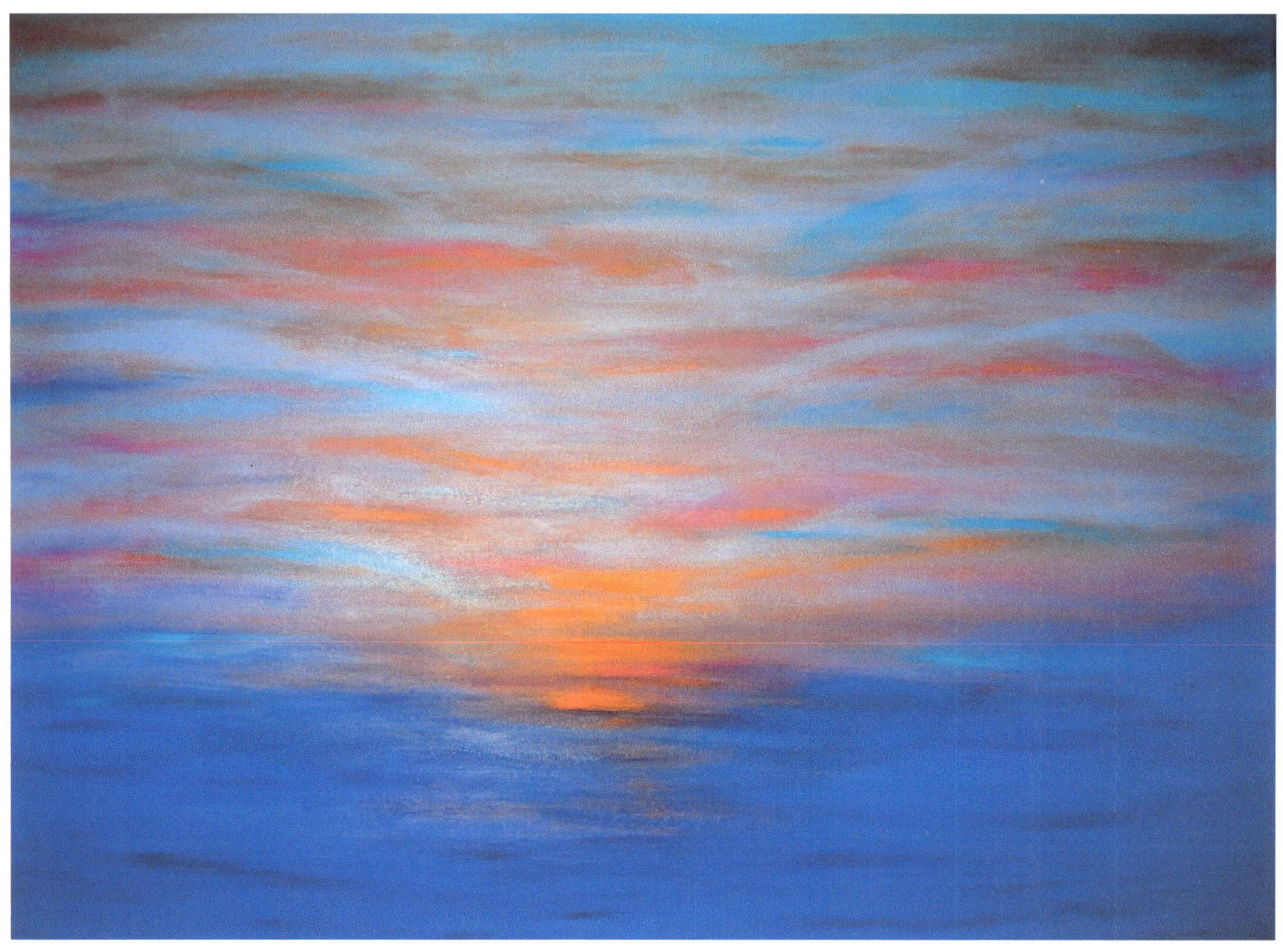

Radiant Dusk, acrylic on canvas, 30 x 40 inches

Streamlined

Reach into your night,
beyond the rays
of turquoise moon,
and into fiery flames
that purify the yearning heart.
No need to complain;
our souls asked
to be streamlined,
to love,
unfettered by fears.
Gaze upon
the un-folding
and the be-coming,
for Grace has fashioned
new eyes
to see the world
and a heart
saturated
in a thousand strands
of light.

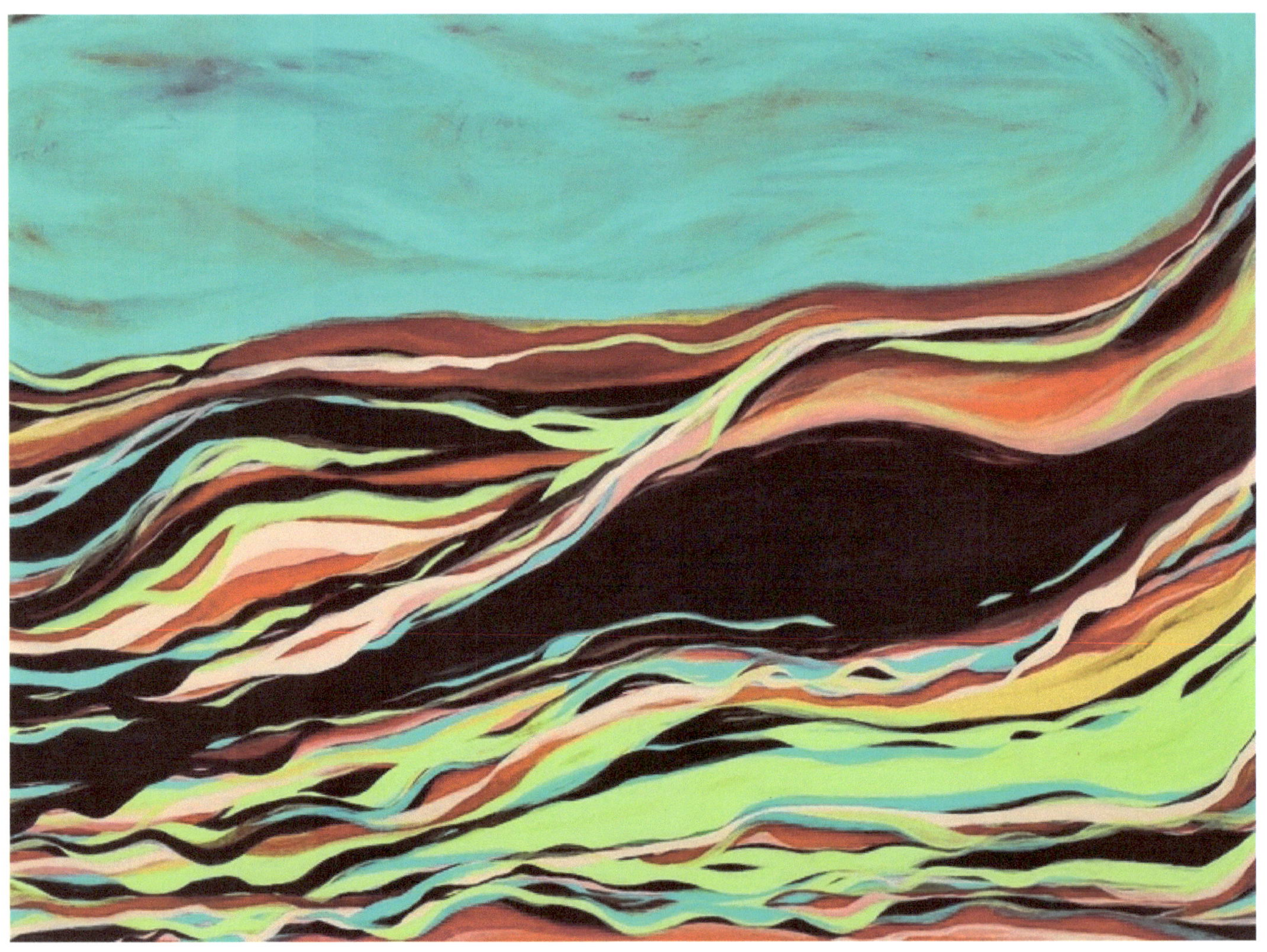

Translucent Wave, acrylic on canvas, 30 x 40 inches

Translucent Wave

Translucent,
inviting,
is the palette of hue,
the sheen of light
that enters each wave,
glowing with the radiance
of sons we glide,
and carried on the hips
of our sisters we stride,
rising,
rising,
under the moon's nudge
and ebbing tide,
we stand among
mystics and lovers,
reaching a union
beyond suffering,
beyond praise,
emptying ourselves
to enter a kiss
inside the sacred center
where wave
becomes bliss.

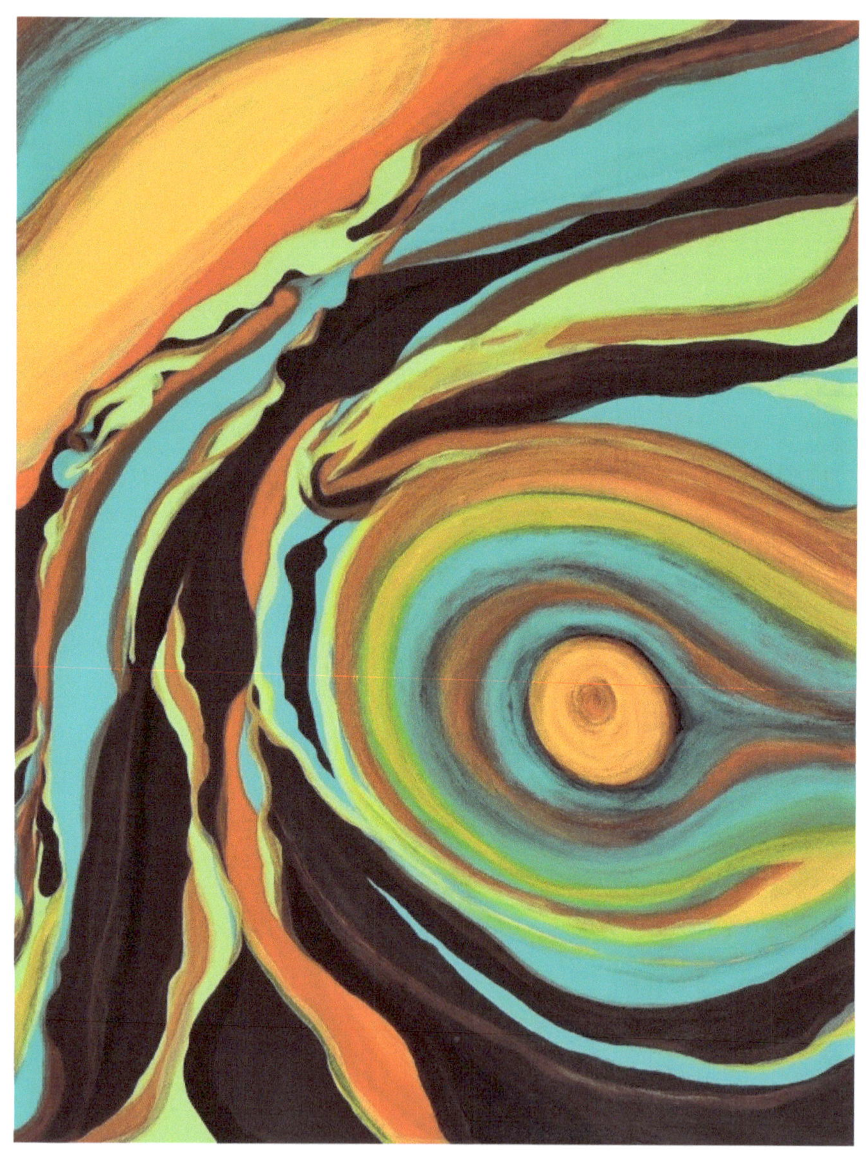

Transparent Courtship, acrylic on canvas, 40 x 30 inches

Transparent Courtship

There is One
that asks us
to remove tired skins,
untold burdens,
and clothes that hide
our true natures.
On this earthly walk,
we hold onto
both worlds
and watch
Love's unseen hand
strengthen us,
help us discern
what is left to learn.
Make time
with your inner
Beloved,
be transparent
in your courtship,
rest and replenish
heart, head, and soul,
and then you will go
places you are led to go,
give in ways that match
your reserves,
and honor souls
that meet you
along the way.
Trust and bend
in the unfolding treasure.
Your Beloved beckons.

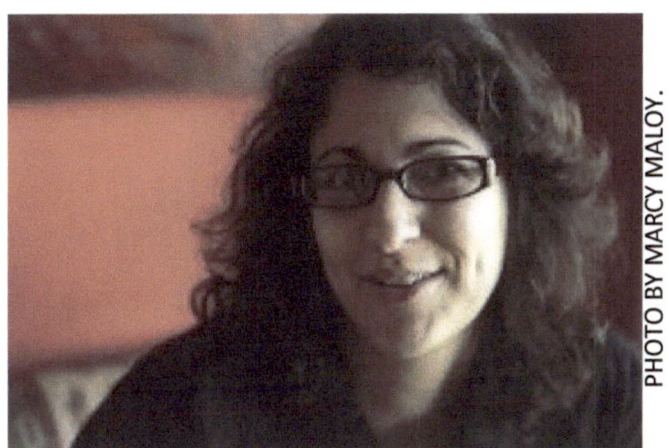

PHOTO BY MARCY MALOY.

ABOUT THE AUTHOR

Tina Karagulian is an artist and poet whose joyful curiosity connects spirituality and creative expression. Her poetry is included in her memoir *It is Time*, *Under the Papaya Tree: A Book of Love Poems,* and *New Skin: Poetry and Prayers*, as well as the following anthologies: *Lifting Women's Voices* and *Sustaining Abundant Life*. *Inner and Outer Space: Paintings and Poetry* is her fourth book published through Black Rose Arts & Press.

www.ingramcontent.com/pod-product-compliance
Lightning Source LLC
LaVergne TN
LVHW070157110826
845147LV00002B/432
9780983804215